Practical Theosophy

By
Annie Besant

Copyright © 2022 Lamp of Trismegistus. All rights reserved. No part of this publication may be reproduced or transmitted in any form or by any means, electronic or mechanical, including photocopying, recording, or by any information storage and retrieval system, without permission in writing from Lamp of Trismegistus. Reviewers may quote brief passages.

ISBN: 978-1-63118-610-3

Esoteric Classics

Other Books in this Series and Related Titles

Aurora of the Philosophers by Paracelsus (978-1-63118-507-6)

Rosicrucian Rules, Secret Signs, Codes and Symbols by various (978-1-63118-488-8)

On the Philadelphian Gold by Philochrysus & Philadelphus (978-1-63118-511-3)

Paracelsus, the Four Elements and Their Spirits by M P Hall (978-1-63118-400-0)

The Stone of the Philosophers by A E Waite (978-1-63118-509-0)

Clairvoyance and Psychic Abilities by A Besant &c (978-1-63118-403-1)

The Rosicrucian Chemical Marriage by Christian Rosenkreuz (978-1-63118-458-1)

The Alchemical Catechism of Paracelsus by Paracelsus (978-1-63118-513-7)

Alchemy in the Nineteenth Century by Helena P. Blavatsky (978-1-63118-446-8)

Rosicrucians and Speculative Masonry in the Seventeenth Century (978-1-63118-489-5)

Qabbalistic Teachings and the Tree of Life by M P Hall (978-1-63118-482-6)

The Sepher Yetzirah and the Qabalah by M P Hall (978-1-63118-481-9)

The Devil in Love by Jacques Cazotte (978–1–63118–499–4)

Fortune-Telling with Dice by Astra Cielo (978-1-63118-466-6)

History, Analysis and Secret Tradition of the Tarot by Hall &c (978-1-63118-445-1)

Crystal Vision Through Crystal Gazing by Frater Achad (978-1-63118-455-0)

The Golden Verses of Pythagoras: Five Translations (978-1-63118-479-6)

Arcane Formulas or Mental Alchemy by W W Atkinson (978-1-63118-459-8)

The Machinery of the Mind by Dion Fortune (978-1-63118-451-2)

The A E Waite Reader: A Selection of Occult Essays (978-1-63118-515-1)

The Leadbeater Reader: A Selection of Occult Essays (978-1-63118-483-3)

Audio versions are also available on Audible, Amazon and Apple

Other Books in this Series and Related Titles

The Human Body in Symbolism by Manly P Hall (978–1–63118–609–7)

Theosophical Basics by William Q Judge (978–1–63118–608–0)

The Hebrew Talisman by Richard Harte (978–1–63118–607–3)

Early Masonic Symbolism by Manly P Hall (978–1–63118–606–6)

Nature Spirits and Elementals by Louise Off (978-1-63118-605-9)

Swedenborg Bifrons by H P Blavatsky (978-1-63118-604-2)

Practical Use of Psychic Powers by C W Leadbeater (978-1-63118-603-5)

Using White & Black Magic by C W Leadbeater (978-1-63118-602-8)

Jesus, the Last Great Initiate by Edouard Schure (978-1-63118-599-1)

Mysterious Wonders of Antiquity by Manly P Hall (978-1-63118-598-4)

Ancient Mysteries and Secret Societies by Manly P Hall (978–1–63118–597–7)

The Zodiac and Its Signs by Manly P Hall (978–1–63118–596–0)

Life and Teachings of Hermes Trismegistus by Manly P Hall (978–1–63118–595–3)

The Secrets of Doctor Taverner by Dion Fortune (978–1–63118–594–6)

Vegetarianism, Theosophy & Occultism by Leadbeater &c (978–1–63118–593–9)

Applied Theosophy by Henry S Olcott (978–1–63118–592–2)

Higher Consciousness by C W Leadbeater (978–1–63118–591–5)

Theories About Reincarnation and Spirits by H P Blavatsky (978–1–63118–590–8)

The Use and Power of Thought by C W Leadbeater (978–1–63118–589–2)

Commentary on the Pymander by G R S Mead (978–1–63118–588–5)

Hypnotism and Mesmerism by Annie Besant (978–1–63118–587–8)

Audio versions are also available on Audible, Amazon and Apple

Table of Contents

Introduction...7

Practical Work For Theosophists...9

Practical Theosophy...14

Theosophy as a Guide in Life...24

Practical Hints For Theosophists...30

Theosophy in Daily Life...36

INTRODUCTION

The word "esoteric" can be difficult to define. Esotericism in general can be seen less as a system of beliefs and more as a category, which encompasses numerous, different systems of beliefs. It's a bit of juxtaposition, since the word "esoteric" indicates something that few people know about, while the term itself broadly covers numerous philosophies, practices, areas of study and belief systems.

In a greater sense, Esotericism acts as a storehouse for secret knowledge, which is often considered ancient (by *tradition, if not by fact),* passed down from generation to generation, in private. At various times in history, simply possessing the knowledge of some of these subjects, was considered illegal and a jailable offence, if discovered. This usually included such general topics as Alchemy, Pharmacology, Qabalah, Hermeticism, Occultism, Ceremonial Magic, Astrology, Divination, Rosicrucianism and so on. Collectively, these areas of study were often referred to as the esoteric sciences.

Sometimes, the outer garment of a subject isn't esoteric, while what is hidden beneath it, is. As an example, Freemasonry isn't necessarily esoteric by nature (at *least not anymore),* but certain signs, passwords and handshakes given to the candidate during their initiation, are in fact, esoteric, in the sense that they are hidden from the general public.

Today, in the twenty-first century, such topics are readily available at bookstores across the country, and numerous main-steam publishers offer beginners guides and coffee-table volumes on many of these subjects, intended for mass appeal. Books like *"The Secret"* have turned previously arcane topics into household knowledge. All that being the case, however, it isn't to say that there still aren't buried secrets to uncover, ancient wisdom being ignored and forgotten mysteries to be explored. In fact, it is often that we are only able to further our own studies by standing on the shoulders of these disappearing giants.

Lamp of Trismegistus is doing its part to help preserve humanity's esoteric history by making some of these classics available to those students who are seeking to unearth the knowledge of these ancient colossi.

So, be sure to check other titles from our *Esoteric Classics* series, as well as our *Occult Fiction, Theosophical Classics, Foundations of Freemasonry Series, Supernatural Fiction, Paranormal Research Series, Studies in Buddhism* and our *Christian Apocrypha Series.* You can also download the audio versions of most of these titles from Amazon, Apple or Audible, for learning on the go.

PRACTICAL WORK FOR THEOSOPHISTS

by Annie Besant

EVERY person who enters the Theosophical Society is bound to accept its first principle, the assertion of the Universal Brotherhood of Man; but it is to be feared that with large numbers of the Fellows the profession remains an empty phrase, too like the "dearly beloved brethren" of the Churches, without bearing on life or effect on conduct. No antithesis can be discovered which is sharper than that between the principle of Brotherhood and the Class-and-Mammon-worship of modern society; no links of true fraternity bind together the dwellers in palaces and the dwellers in slums; no golden bands of sympathy unite the wealthy and the poor. Yet Altruism remains only a name so long as it is severed from personal service of Humanity, and Theosophy is merely a new form of glorified selfishness for those who " take it up " from curiosity, or from the desire to know, merely that the knowledge may be a personal possession and powers be attained for the sake of wielding them. At the great gate of the Temple of Knowledge stands the Guardian, and if to his question: " Why dost thou desire to know and to achieve ?" there comes any answer but : "That I may the better serve Humanity", the candidate for admission should be sent back to his spelling book, until he has learned the alphabet of Altruism.

Let us suppose that all the latent powers of the Human Intellect and Will could suddenly be developed in the men and the women around us as by the touch of a magician's wand, and that they could step forth into the world clothed with supersensual knowledge and power; what would it avail, save to make this world a worse hell of contending passions than it is today, in which would rage Titanic contests of selfishness and greed, rendered the more horrible by the mightier powers of those engaged in the fratricidal struggle? Not until the brute in us is starved out of life; not until the lower self is slain and only the voice of the Higher Self is heard; not until personal desire has been lost in the desire for humanity; not until all ambition is dead, save the ambition to serve; not until this point is reached can power be safely trusted in human hands. Those who lightly enter the Theosophical Society, imagining that thereby they will at once spring into the exercise of the higher human capabilities, have to learn that the capacity to lead the Higher Life must precede the capacity to wield the higher powers. Hence the long probation insisted on for every candidate; the deep study which ensures that knowledge shall precede Power; the tests which bar the way towards the higher planes of being. And since character grows out of habits, and habits out of acts often repeated, there is no better school for forming habits of unselfishness, no surer way of moulding the selfless character, than by doing personal acts of service to our brothers and sisters struggling in the sad environment made for them by our modern civilization.

First must come the real honest feeling of equality, not the verbal profession, but the inner conviction. Unless this exists, all work among the poor tends to become demoralising both to helper and to helped, breeding self-complacency in the one and subserviency in the other. Every act must spring spontaneously from the brotherly relationship; so that aid, comfort, counsel, whenever given, shall be the free and loving gift of brother to brother, so that respect of the highest in the lowest shall breed self-respect, and charity, in re-becoming Love, shall purify and raise and not degrade. But, I repeat, the feeling of equality must be real, all social castes merging into the human brotherhood, so that there is no consciousness of difference whether speaking to prince or pauper, the man and the woman becoming everything and the rank nothing.

Then comes the cleansing of one's own life in its relations to those by whose labour we are fed and clothed and housed. Every article that we use embodies so much human labour, and if we use it, we are bound to render back for it due equivalent of our own labour. If this be not done, we are robbing instead of exchanging, soiling our lives by theft. And here I speak to Theosophists belonging to the "middle" and "upper" classes, for the poor, already crushed by labour, are forced to buy what they need for subsistence at the lowest rate at which they can obtain it. This is not so among the richer, and they are bound to see that they do not vicariously sweat the workers by their purchases of "cheap goods". In this matter women are the worst sinners, buying gowns and other articles of clothing at prices which they know cannot cover the cost of material and a fair wage to the needlewoman. If they would personally employ the needlewoman instead of buying her work from the shop, they would not dare to pay her the starvation wage which they pay her through the hands of the middlemen; and they would not then be wearing garments soiled perhaps by the harlotry which has been fled to for a piece of bread. If they cannot manage this personal employment, they can easily ascertain who are fair and who are unfair employers by writing for information to Miss Clementina Black, 198, High Holborn, London, W.C., who has exerted herself to form a Consumers' League of persons ashamed to live by sweating their neighbours. It is hardly necessary to add that the personal life of the Theosophist should be frugal, simple, and free from luxury, both for the sake of his own inner development, and in order that he may live honestly, not taking more than he gives.

The personal life thus purified, there remains the active service due to our fellows. Each must here judge his own capacities and opportunities, but there are two or three lines of work in which painstaking and cultured men and women are much wanted at the present time. For instance, some might serve as managers of our Board Schools, attending to the remission of fees, supervising the tone and method of instruction, noting if the children are properly fed, organizing free meals for those in need, and giving to the teachers the sympathy and friendliness which they so sorely lack in their arduous and responsible labour. There are openings for useful and far-reaching service in this line of work second, perhaps, to none, bearing as it does on the training of the citizens of the future as well as on lightening the burdens that press so heavily today.

Women, with leisure on their hands, can find away of using that leisure in the service of others by writing to Allen D. Graham, 18, Buckingham Street, Strand. Mr. Graham, some time ago, finding that invalided children were constantly being sent from the hospitals to poor, overcrowded, and often dirty homes, suggested that kind-hearted folk might each take charge of two or three of such children, visiting them, playing with them, taking them out, and, in fact, generally "mothering" them. These little ones, ailing and feeble, suffer terribly in this rough hurrying world, and much pain might be saved, much pleasure given, by a little sacrifice of time and trouble.

Another form of service, open to the wealthier, is buying shares in companies whose servants are notoriously overworked, and then attending the shareholders' meetings and insisting on shorter hours, higher wages, and better treatment all round. The dividends from the shares can be paid into the Union fund of the employees where a Trade Union exists; where there is no Trade Union, no more useful work can be done than urging the men or women to unite and aiding them in the first uphill steps of organization.

These suggestions ma y serve as examples of the kind of service which is crying aloud to be done, of practical profession of the Brotherhood of Man. I am not putting them forward as remedies for the evils inseparable from the present order of Society. As a Socialist, I know but too well that all such work as this can only act as palliative, not as cure; none the less will it lighten some of the darkness around us, and, in the absence of the sun, farthing dips are better than unbroken Cimmerian gloom.

It is obvious that, in addition to such duteous Service of Man as I have been glancing at, there are other duties incumbent on every member of the T. S.. Those who can use their pens should answer objections or expose slanders made in the columns of our ordinary press; most editors will put in a tersely-written clear reply to attacks made in their papers. And all should study Theosophical teachings, both for their own culture and for the assistance of others. It is not enough to set our own feet on the Path; as soon as we are able we should guide thitherward the feet of others; and in order that we may be competent for the task, we must study, study, study. The subtle metaphysics of Theosophy will attract but the few; few, again, are likely to feel the call to climb the rugged path to those heights on which the Masters sit serene. Neither its philosophy nor its possibilities of growth will avail much to recommend it to the superficial thinkers or to the luxurious livers of our day. But the sight of noble lives, strenuously and selflessly working for human good, battling against poverty and sorrow, the twin-daughters of Ignorance, these will justify Theosophy in the eyes of the world, proving that self-devotion can exist apart from superstition, that clear-eyed Intellect can walk hand-in-hand with the Love that saves.

PRACTICAL THEOSOPHY

by Anon

WE hear a good deal at present about "Practical Theosophy". Is such a thing possible? If so, in what does it exist? To many Theosophists, Theosophy is an individual internal thing, a system of cosmogony, philosophy, ontology, to which the term *practical* is completely inapplicable. As well, they think, talk of practical metaphysics! Others, again, feel that to love your neighbour and still neglect to help him in the material things in which your aid would evidently be to his advantage, is a barren mockery. One meets people continually who hardly stir a finger to help others, and yet who talk glibly about the "Rounds" and the "Rings", and the "seven principles" of man; who long for Nirvana, even for Paranirvana; who ardently desire to be joined to the infinite, absorbed into the eternal; who feel that all men are their brothers, all women their sisters, and that thought makes them oh! so happy, gives them such peace of mind! The convict is their brother — their caught and locked-up brother — the tramp is their brother — their idle, unwashed, whisky-soaked, good-for-nothing brother; the workwoman is their sister — their poor, friendless sister, who has to sew sixteen hours a day to keep body and soul together; even the prostitute is their sister — their fallen, wicked sister, who is hurrying to an early grave; the famine-stricken Irish, Chinese, Hindus, are their brothers and sisters — their skin-and-bone brothers and sisters, who are dying of starvation. Theosophy teaches them these beautiful truths, they say, and it does them so much good to know it all! Speak to these sentimentalists about "Practical Theosophy", and they look suddenly stupid. *Tell* them that in a garret not a hundred yards from their back door there lies a fever-stricken family — that you know of fifty cases of genuine distress that they could aid by their money and sympathy, and they look at you as if you were something they had eaten which had not agreed with them. Perhaps they tell you that Theosophy is a spiritual affair, something of a private and confidential nature between their "higher selves " and the Great All, into which no vulgar, earthly considerations enter. These people are probably quite unaware what a wretched sham their "Theosophy " is, and what miserable frauds they are themselves when they pose as Theosophists. They don't know they are selfish. It has never entered their heads to think what would be their thoughts, their words and their actions if they really felt what they say they feel, if they realized in their hearts the meaning of the words "my brother", "my sister".

These people do not trouble themselves to think what their sentiments would be did they learn that a real brother or sister was in want of their aid. Suppose they heard some fine morning that their brother was starving to death, without the means of procuring food, what would be their sensations? Would not their hearts stop beating in horror ? Would not every nerve tingle with excitement and with anxiety to save him? What pictures their imagination would draw! Their beloved brother lying helpless on the floor of some wretched hut, while the wife he loved and the children of his heart, emaciated to skeletons like himself, lay dead or dying around him. Would not any woman under these circumstances fly to her banker and make him instantly telegraph money to his agents in the nearest town, with instructions to send messengers at any cost to her brother with immediate relief ? Were she a poor woman, would she not hurry with her trinkets, her clothes, her furniture, anything, to the poor man's banker, the pawnbroker, thankful and proud to be able thus to raise the money to save her brother and his family from horrible death ? And then what feverish anxiety, what sleepless nights, until she learned that the relief she had sent had reached her brother in time! Or, Suppose a man were told that his pure and innocent sister had been morally tripped up and socially knocked down by some selfish brute whom she had trusted — had been psychically drugged by him, "ruined," deserted, cast out, reviled and spat upon by people morally and intellectually unworthy to be her scullions; handed over in cold blood by the "moral" and the "pious" to the tender mercies of the most selfish and most brutal of both sexes, to be trampled hopelessly into the mud, the helpless slave of the demons of drink and lust. Would not every spark of manliness in him be fanned into a blaze of indignation and rage ? Would he not employ every conceivable means to discover the poor girl's hiding-place ? And when he had found his sister, would he not throw his protecting arm around her and fight his way with her out of the hyena's den, past the toads of scandal and the vipers of malice, and give her an asylum in his heart and hearth, where the poor wounded, terrified, half-demented girl could recover her mental, moral and physical health; while those who had never tripped, or who had never been seen to fall, howled, and snarled, and hissed, and grimaced before his door in impotent rage that a victim had been rescued from the hell to which they had consigned her as a sacrifice to their demon-god — the great infernal trinity of hypocrisy, cruelty and selfishness ?

No! those who descant upon the brotherhood of man seldom realize, even in the faintest degree, the meaning of the pretty sentimental words they utter. If they did, there would be no question as to the nature of Practical Theosophy. If they did, a great unrest would seize them, a supreme desire to help the thousands of suffering brothers and sisters that cross their path every day of their lives, and from whom they shrink because cowardice, selfishness, and indolence inhabit furnished lodgings in their hearts.

The Australian savage murders any black-fellows he meets who do not belong to his little tribe. He kills them on general principles — because they belong to "another set". The civilized world has advanced so far upon the road to Practical Theosophy, that we do not actually murder or maim those who do not belong to our tribe, we merely let them suffer and die, and the advanced ones, the pioneers of the race, write on their tomb-stones, "Here lie my dear brothers and sisters".

The fact is, however, and a staggering one it is too, that Practical Theosophy, in its full acceptation, would mean a dissolution of society as at present constituted. Of that fact there cannot be the slightest doubt, for it would mean a reign of kindness, of sympathy, of unselfishness, of tenderness to the weak, of forgiveness for the erring, of mutual helpfulness, of happiness in seeing others happy, and there is not a single one of our present social institutions that is not founded upon principles diametrically the opposite of these, and which would not swell up and burst to pieces were the ferment of altruism introduced into it. Only fancy what the result would be of introducing Practical Theosophy into our treatment of criminals, and into our legal processes. What would become of that dignified and learned profession, the law, were the object of the solicitor and the barrister to make people friendly and forgiving, instead of being to fan their enmity, spite and hatred ? What would we do with our great prisons and convict establishments, were jurymen, judges and legislators to really look upon criminals as their ignorant, misguided, erring, stupid, neglected brothers and sisters ? Or, again, what would become of our arsenals and iron-clads, of our generals and admirals, our colonels and captains, and our be-feathered and be-belted warriors generally, were the people of various nationalities to refuse to shoot and stab and blow each other to pieces at the word of command, for no better reason than that they were brothers and had no quarrel, and did not want to harm each other, or each other's wives or children ? Another noble profession would go to the dogs ! What would become of the churches were the clergy to treat their fellow-creatures as brothers and sisters ? Would not the bishops hasten to convert their palaces into asylums for the homeless wretches who now lie shivering at night in the road before their gates ? Would not the lesser clergy quickly follow their example ? Then they would have to feed these unfortunates, for the bishop's brothers and sisters are starving all the time as well as shivering; and how could they do that and at the same time maintain au establishment ? What would the Lord think of His ministers if they neglected to keep up their place in society ? The next thing would probably be that the clergy would open their great empty churches for wretched and homeless women and children to take shelter in, instead of letting them lie shivering in the rain and wind before the barred doors of those gloomy temples of their jealous God — and then what on earth would become of religion?

But let us be reassured! The social order is in no danger just yet of being upset by the introduction of Practical Theosophy into the lives of men. Practical Theosophy to exist, except in fancy, requires Practical Theosophists — in other words, people who value the happiness of others more than their own enjoyments, and such people are a rare exception in any place in life — in the law the army, the church, the legislature, in agriculture, trade, commerce or manufacture. If anyone feels today that his sentiments are those of Practical Theosophy, and seriously proposes to sacrifice his worldly prospects and enjoyments in order to spend his life in doing what little he can to benefit others, he runs a risk, that is not far from a certainty, of being treated by the world as all incorrigible lunatic. It is a fact which few will deny that anyone would be considered a madman who openly and confessedly followed the injunction of the great Practical Theosophist of Judea, to sell all that he had, and having given the proceeds to the poor, to follow him — that is to say, who devoted his life, in complete forgetfulness of self, to the great and glorious task of raising humanity out of the quagmire of ignorance, selfishness and cruelty, in which it flounders. If he had some reasonable object in view, well and good. The world can understand a person being altruistic for the sake of a good living and an assured position in society — there is some sense in that; it can even excuse a man for loving his neighbours, if he firmly believes that he will thereby be entitled to a reserved seat in the hall of the gods; but "utter forgetfulness of self", that is quite unnatural, and amounts to a sign of weakness of intellect!

When people talk of Practical Theosophy as a thing that is possible in the world today, in ninety-nine cases out of a hundred they are thinking of practical benevolence and charity; for if the very foundation of Theosophy be the sentiment of the brotherhood of man, Practical Theosophy, by the very laws of society, as at present constituted, is an impossibility. Law, religion, politics, our very system of morality itself, are all incompatible with the existence of the sentiment of the brotherhood of man. All these institutions were invented by and for people imbued with the opposite sentiments; they are fitted only for such people, and could not exist for ten minutes in a world inhabited by Practical Theosophists.

The natural laws that govern the manifestations of Practical Theosophy are as different to those that obtain in our present system of egoism and destructive competition, as the laws that govern the phenomena of steam are to the laws of hydraulics. We know full well that no steam will be generated in a boiler until the whole of the water therein has been raised to boiling-point. Even so we also know that in order to raise the world to the point at which men will "generate", Practical Theosophy, the spiritual temperature of the whole of mankind, must be raised; all men and women must be made kinder and still kinder in heart, and stronger and still stronger in spirit; and this call only be done by acting on them *en masse*, and raising the standard of kindness and of spiritual strength in the whole race.

Will works of benevolence and charity do this ? Are they not in themselves a consequence rather than a cause, a fruit rather than a seed ? Such works are indeed a fruit, the immature fruit which the tree of kindness bears in the half-grown stunted condition it necessarily presents when planted in the uncongenial soil of selfishness. Benevolence and charity belong to the time when men stone and crucify those who tell them that all men are brothers and ought to treat each other as such. They are the tithe grudgingly paid by vice to virtue, by egoism to altruism, and their existence shows that egoism and vice take nine- tenths, or rather ninety-nine hundredths, of the produce of human life. Were Practical Theosophy the rule of life, benevolence and charity would not be needed, for they owe their existence to the greater prevalence of malevolence and injustice. They are the exceptions occurring when the rule is in force, and disappear when the rule ceases to act. Benevolence has become an anachronism since the idea of universal brotherhood dawned upon the world. Charity, under the higher law, is no better than a flattering deceiver, for it tells people that they are worthy of praise and reward for doing the things which Theosophy declares it to be criminal to leave undone, because not to do them, and a thousand times more, is to do injustice. Active works of benevolence and charity are therefore not Practical Theosophy. They belong to the old regime of egoism, of which they are the flowers and the fruit; and, however good in themselves, they should not be mistaken for Practical Theosophy if a dangerous delusion is to be avoided.

If, then, Practical Theosophy be in reality a form of human life — of morality and of society — far higher than those which exist in the world of today, and for the coming of which we can but prepare the way, can we, nevertheless, not give a practical turn to such Theosophy as we already have, so that it will hurry on the reign of Brotherhood ? Or must our Theosophy remain for long centuries only a self-centred and self-ideal thing ? What form can we Theosophists give to our efforts as to make our Theosophy an influence in the world for good ? If Theosophy is to be the guiding power of our lives, in what manner, and to what end, is it to guide us?

We cannot, at the present day, exercise Practical Theosophy and still remain in such harmony with our surroundings as would entitle us in the world's eyes to be called sane. We cannot even realize in our imagination, soaked through as we are with egotistic modes of thought and standards of value, what it will be like to live in a world peopled by Practical Theosophists. But, without the slightest doubt, we can turn what Theosophy we have in us to practical account; for we can each of us add his or her warmth to the general heat, and thus help to raise the moral and spiritual temperature of the world a little nearer to the point at which the free generation of Practical Theosophy will naturally take place among men. We must remember, however, that for the exercise of Practical Theosophy, as it will one day exist in the world, reciprocity is necessary. If the person you treat as a brother treats you in return as an enemy, the real effect of the principle of Brotherhood cannot manifest itself; and at present, as society is constituted, it is not possible, and not in human nature, for any man to carry out that principle in all his intercourse with his neighbours. Practical Theosophy in isolated individuals, if it is to avoid an opposition that would paralyse or destroy it, must of necessity take on a somewhat different form to that it would assume in a society where all were Practical Theosophists.

The Practical Theosophist of today is the individual who is animated by that spirit of brotherhood which will one day become universal; and, as such, he is none other than the man who at all times tries to impart to others the Theosophical knowledge he has got himself, and to imbue them with the Theosophical principles by which he guides his own conduct; who tries to stir up in others the spirit of kindness, of patience, of gentleness, of courage and of truth; who tries to induce his neighbours fearlessly to think out the problem of existence for themselves, and to feel the dignity and the responsibility of their own manhood and womanhood; who tries to make others self-respecting and strong. Those who become penetrated by these sentiments and qualities do not need any stimulus to make them engage in works of so-called charity, for these will be for them the natural outlet, in the present order of things, for their overflowing impulse to benefit others. The feelings that prompt to all kind actions belong to the domain of Practical Theosophy, but the actual works of benevolence and charity to which they prompt are not Theosophy; they are accidents in the growth of Theosophy, just as the useful inventions of modern times are accidents in the progress of Science. The object of Science is not to discover new bleaching powders, or murderous explosives; its object is the intellectual conquest of material nature. Even so the object of Theosophy is the moral conquest of man's animal nature, irrespective of the soup kitchens and orphan asylums that spring up during the process. It seeks to subdue or chase out the toad, the vulture, the wolf, the pig, the viper, the sloth, the shark, and all the rest of the menagerie of lower animal natures that now howl and croak and hiss and grunt and caw in the hearts of men, and it knows that this is an operation which can only be performed by each man for himself. Each must purify his own mind and make his own spirit strong, and the difference between Theoretical and Practical Theosophists is that the former talk about these things and the latter do them. But though this process is a self-regarding one, the effect is not. He who is a Practical Theosophist, who tries to make himself strong and pure-hearted, is, even unconsciously, a powerful influence in the world, and he becomes a centre of energy potent in proportion as he forgets himself, and merges his hopes and fears, his likes and dislikes, his thoughts, words, and deeds, in the great life of humanity — dissolving his personality, so to say, in the race to which he belongs; feeling with it, thinking for it, bearing its burdens in his consciousness, and its sins upon his conscience; and knowing that to sacrifice himself for the good of humanity is therefore in reality but to ensure his own salvation.

The Practical Theosophist, in proportion to his own strength, gives strength to all with whom he comes in contact, through a process somewhat similar to that of electrical induction. Colonel Ingersoll was once asked if he thought he could improve upon the work of "the Creator". He replied that had he been consulted he would have made good health catching, instead of disease. Had the great American orator and wit looked a little deeper into his own heart, he would have seen that "the Creator" is not so stupid as he thinks Him, for health is in reality catching, especially health of mind and heart; and Ingersoll himself owes most of his great influence in the world of thought, not to his logic, powerful as that is, not to his wonderful command of illustrations and similes, not to his rapid flow of brilliant language, but to the healthy contagion of a heart overflowing with the magnetism of kindness, generosity and pity, and charged with the electricity of a love for the good, the true and the beautiful. The Practical Theosophist, wherever he goes and whatever he does, causes those with whom he has to do to "catch" Theosophy. A hint dropped here, a word said there, a question asked, an opinion expressed, become through the power of his vitalizing magnetism the seeds of Theosophy in others.

Practical Theosophy then is the sum of those institutions into which human life will spontaneously crystalize when men and women become Practical Theosophists; in other words, when they feel in their hearts that all men are brothers, and act accordingly. Practical Theosophists today, those sporadic and premature instances of all altruism that will one day become universal, are the drops that precede and presage the rain. They cannot, under the rule of the present morality, and with existing social religious and political institutions, live and act as they would were all men as they themselves are. The most they can hope to do is to try their best to prepare the world for the reception of human brotherhood as the foundation of all our ideas of life and morality; and this they can best accomplish by each one making himself pure and strong, for then they become centres of a spiritual health which is "catching"; they become laya points", so to say, through which there flows into the world from another plane of existence the spirit of brotherhood, of mercy, of pity and of love.

Practical Theosophy is the great edifice which will be constructed here below by the invisible, intelligent Powers of Nature as soon as there exists on earth the material necessary to build it. Practical Theosophists are the bricks with which the edifice will one day be constructed; and the builders only wait until the lumps of mud that now cover the earth have been converted by the fire of misery and sorrow, of painful effort and sustained aspiration, into hard and shining bricks, fit to build a temple to the living God.

THEOSOPHY AS A GUIDE IN LIFE

by Anon

THIS is a practical age, and every system or theory is challenged to give proofs of what it may accomplish in action. How very little is gained by mere belief is the standing reproach to Churches. Their diversified Creeds have been steadily evolving through the centuries as new problems in theology or science arose, and today the separated sects have an outfit of every possible belief on every possible theme. No small proportion of these themes are in regions remote from practical life, as also from any means of proof. They concern such questions as the number and nature of Divine Beings, the character and bearing of the Divine Will, the fixedness of the future life, the best form of ecclesiastical sacraments, — all of them with little facility of demonstration and with no utility when demonstrated. Moreover, it is quite evident that, whether there be One God or Three, whether He predestinates or not, whether evil-doers are damned eternally or temporarily, whether Baptism is efficacious towards pardon, the various sects have not made this earth more worthy of the Divine care or diminished the evils which religion should cure. As conservators of morals, abaters of sin, regenerators of society, Churches are assuredly a lamentable failure. It is not merely that society remains unregenerated, but that nobody now expects them to regenerate it. A copious provision of minute creeds has clearly done nothing to extirpate evil.

This being so, it is just as certain that the addition of another creed will not do so. The two classes interested in human progress are the philanthropic and the devout, and both, when any unfamiliar scheme for such progress is submitted to them, are sure to point out that mere beliefs have wholly failed. They say, with entire correctness, that not a new platform or Church is heeded, but something with an object and an impulsion hitherto untried. If Theosophy has no better aim than have the sects, if it imparts no motive stronger than do they, if it can show no results more distinct and valuable, it may as well be rejected now as after a futile trial. But, on the other hand, if it holds out a better prospect and a finer spur, if it can prove that these have actually operated where conventional ones have failed, it is entitled to a hearing. The doctrinal question is subordinate, though, of course, an ethical system is more hopeful if upon a rational basis.

Let us see if the unfamiliar system known as "Theosophy", and which has lately received so much attention from the thinking world, possesses any qualities warranting its substitution for the religions around it. They have not reformed mankind; can It?

Now 1st.—*Theosophy abolishes the cause of all of the sin, and most of the misery of life.* That cause is selfishness. Every form of dishonesty, violence, outrage, fraud, even discourtesy, comes from the desire to promote one's own ends, even if the rights of others have to be sacrificed thereby. All aggression upon fellow-men, all attempts to appropriate their comfort, possessions, or plans, all efforts to belittle, outshine, or humiliate them, express the feeling that self-gratification is to be sought before all else. This is equally true of personal vices, as well as of that personal contempt for Divine authority which we may call "impiety". Hence the root of all evil conduct towards God, towards other men, or towards one-self is self-love, self-love so strong as to sacrifice everything rather than its own indulgence.

From this indulgence follow two things. First, the pains of envy, disappointment, jealousy, and all the mean and biting passions which attend the ever-present thought of self; and the utter loss of all those finer, gentler joys which are the fruit of beneficence and altruism. Second, the restraining measures which society, for its own protection, is obliged to put upon aggression in its coarser forms — the workhouses, jails, and gibbets from which no land of civilization and churches is free. And if we wish to realize what would be the effect of a universal reign of unselfishness among men, we may picture a land without courts, prisons, and policemen, a society without peculation, chicanery, or deceit, a community whereof every heart was as vacant of envy and guile as it certainly would be of unhappiness and pain. The root of universal sorrow would be eradicated, the stream dried at its source.

Now this is what Theosophy enjoins. Its cardinal doctrine is the absolute equality of human rights and the universal obligation to respect them. If my neighbour's possessions — of feeling, property, happiness, what not — are as much to be regarded as are mine, and if I feel that, I shall not invade them. Still more. If I perceive the true fraternity of man, if I am in accord with the law of sympathy it evokes, if I realize that the richest pleasure comes from giving rather than receiving good, I shall hot be passively unaggressive, I shall be actively beneficent. In other words, I shall be a true philanthropist. And in being this I shall have gained the highest reach of happiness to self, for " he that loseth his life, the same shall save it." You say that this is a Christian text ? Very well; it is also the epitome of Theosophy.

Then 2nd —*Theosophy so tends ceaselessly the truth that every act of right or wrong shall receive its due reward.* Most religious systems say otherwise. Usually they provide a "vicarious" plan by which punishment is to be dodged and unearned bliss secured. But if awards may be transferred, so may duties, and thus chaos is introduced into the moral order of the universe. Moreover, the palpable injustices of human life, those injustices which grieve the loving heart and sting the bitter one, are unaccounted for. All the inequalities and paradoxes and uncertainties so thick around us are insoluble. *Why* evil flourishes and good withers may not be known. Night settles down on the most important of human questions.

Theosophy illuminates it at once. It insists that moral causes are no less effective than are physical, and that its due effect, in harm or benefit, is infallibly attached to every moral act. There is no escape, no loss, no uncertainty; the law is absolutely unflinching and irresistible.

Every penny of debt must be paid, by or to the individual himself. Not by any means necessarily in one life, but somewhere and somehow along the great chain is rigorous justice done; for the effect of causes generated on the moral plane may have to exhaust themselves in physical circumstances.

If unselfishness constitutes the method towards social regeneration, Karma — for such is the name of this doctrine of justice — must constitute its stimulus. Nothing fails — no good, no evil, can die without its fruit. The result of a deed is as certain as the deed. How can a system be unpractical when it abolishes every bar to the law of causation, and makes practice the key to its whole operation?

Then 3rd .— *Theosophy holds that every man is the framer of his own destiny.* All the theological apparatus of "elections", and "predestinations", and "foreordinations" it breaks indignantly to bits. The semi-material theories of "luck", and "fate", and "chance" fare no better. Every other theory which shifts responsibility or paralyzes effort is swept away. Theosophy will have none of them. It insists that we can be only that which we have willed to be, that no power above or below will thwart or divert us, that our destiny is in our own hands. We may perceive the beauty of that conception of the future which embodies it in a restoration to the Divine fulness through continuous purgation of all that is sensuous and selfish and belittling, and, so perceiving, may struggle on towards that distant goal; or self- besotted, eager only for the transient and the material, we may hug closely our present joys, heedless alike of others and of Karmic law; but, whatever be the ideal, whatever the effort, whatever the result, it is ours alone. No Divinity will greet the conqueror as a favourite of Heaven; no Demon will seize the lost in a pre-destined clutch. What we are we have made ourselves; what we shall be is ours to make.

Here comes in the fact of Re-incarnation. No one life is adequate to a man's development. Again and again must he come to earth, to taste its quality, to lay up its experience and its discipline, each career on earth determining the nature of its successor. Two things follow: 1st, our present state discloses what we have accomplished in past lives; 2nd, our present habits decide what the next life shall be. The formative power is lodged in us; our aspiration prompting, our will effecting, the aim desired. Surely it is the perfection of fairness that every man shall be what he wishes to be!

Of all the many schemes for human melioration which history has recorded and humanity tried, is there one so rational, so just, so impartial, so elevating, so motived, as that presented by Theosophy ? Artificial distinctions and conceptions are wholly expunged. Fanciful ambitions have absolutely no place. Mechanical devices are completely absent. The root of all separations and enmities — selfishness — is exposed and denounced. The inflexibility of moral law is vigorously declaimed. The realization of individual aim is made entirely individual. Thus sweeping away every artifice and annulling every check devised by theologians, opening the path to the highest ideal of religious fervour, insuring that not an item is lost in the long account each man runs up in his many lives, handing over to each the determination and the acquirement of his chosen aim, Theosophy does what no rival system has done or can do — affirms the moral consciousness, vindicates the moral sense, spurs the moral motive. And thus it is both practical and practicable.

Thus, too, it becomes a guide in life. Once given the aim before a man and the certainty that every act affects that aim, the question of the expediency of any act is at once determined. Is an act selfish, unfraternal, aggressive? It is then untheosophical. Is it conducive to unselfishness, spirituality, progress? Then Theosophy affirms it. The test is simple and uncomplicated, and, because so, feasible. He who would be guided through the intricacies of life need seek no priest or intercessor, but, illuminated with the Divine Spirit ever present in his inner man, stimulated by the vision of ultimate reunion with the Supreme, assured that each effort has its inseparately-joined result, conscious that in himself is the responsibility for its an adoption, may go on in harmony, hope, and happiness, free from misgivings as to justice or success, and strong in the faith that he who has conformed to Nature and her laws shall be conformed to the destiny which she predicts for *Man*.

PRACTICAL HINTS FOR THEOSOPHISTS

by Kate E. Mills

THERE are probably hundreds of sincere members of the Theosophical Society who are willing and anxious to help "the cause", who yet, from one hindrance or another, find, when they balance their yearly accounts, that they have not given a solitary five-pound-note to help the work which, as "Fellows", they must have so much at heart. This is naturally distressing to them as individuals, and hurtful to the society at large, in that it cramps its power for usefulness.

How can this state of things be altered?

We all feel that it is humiliating to us as members of this Society to reflect that money is not forthcoming to carry on an energetic propagandism, to know that even the least expensive, most necessary, and most popular method of awakening public interest, is threatened with extinction for want of funds, and that the support which is received by the Society's English official organ, "Lucifer", comes from outsiders, and not, as it should do, from those who have sufficiently appreciated the importance of Theosophical teaching to solicit the privilege of joining the greatest reformatory movement that has arisen since Jesus of Nazareth preached to an unheeding world.

But it is want of knowledge, want of thought, that is answerable for the unsatisfactory state of the treasury of the Theosophical Society. It has been taken for granted that all members must know how much money is needed to carry on an active war against the crass materialism that is eating the spiritual life out of Western nations. Now, it is quite possible that very many have not known, that very many do not even now know, how much the cause is hindered for lack of pence.

It has been taken for granted that all members would have enough common-sense to divine the wants of the war chest. But common sense is a most rare possession. Possibly commonsense and thoughtfulness might have been enough to enlighten us, but we belong to a nation that is not slow to make its wants known, and when no one asks us to put our hands in our purses we come to the conclusion that the contents thereof are not desired.

So it has come to pass that this one and that one has had a subscription, while the Theosophical Society and its needs have been overlooked and forgotten. We very much reverse the children's saying: "Those that ask must not have", though we show our faith in the witty rejoinder, "Those that don't ask don't want".

But the ice has been broken, an authoritative statement has been made, and all members ought by this time to be aware that money is urgently needed, and knowing this they ought to make it their personal business to see that the coffers are well supplied with the requisite funds for keeping up an active propaganda.

We will suppose, for politeness sake, that the means at the command of the "Fellows" is strictly limited. We will suppose, for the sake of courtesy that the majority of the members of the T. S. are poor; but it is a supposition requiring a great deal of courtesy to cover it, as the teaching of Theosophy in its present stage scarcely appeals to the indigent. The question, then, before us is, " How are poor 'Fellows' to spare money to carry on the work they believe to be of supreme importance to the human race?"

It would be an insult to suggest that anyone whose eyes have been opened to a wider range of vision, from whose heart has fallen the weight of hopeless oppression, that the seeming injustice of the scheme of creation as taught by the churches imposed, can be indifferent to the diffusion of that knowledge which has conferred upon him so priceless a blessing.

We dare not think our brothers indifferent, but we may suppose them to be poor. What can the poor do, and how can they do it?

The present writer would be very sorry to say anything disagreeable, or to draw odious comparisons, and, being a F. T. S., may be allowed to think that the members of the Theosophical Society are, as a body, vastly superior to the members of any other society whatever, much more to the humble, ignorant "Salvationists", yet — from the self-denial of these poor, unlettered, ranting, rollicking "lads" and "lasses", who are, many of them, only half fed at the best of times, the "Army" received as the proceeds of this year's (1889) "Denial Week" no less a sum than twenty thousand and forty-one pounds. "How is it accomplished by those who only have bare necessities?" was asked a pleasant-faced Salvationist.

"Well, you see, one goes without sugar, another without tea or meat, or may be without both, for 'Denial Week', and sends the money these would have cost to the General."

Self-denial is an article in the Theosophist's creed. Shall we show wisdom in refusing to take a hint from those whose methods, I fear, too many of us are inclined to despise? What if we made our self-denial extend over the three hundred and sixty-five days of the year? What if we took to heart this world's woes? What if we desire its enlightenment as earnestly as these children of privation and toil desire, what they believe to be, its salvation? Would it be necessary for our reverenced teacher to remind us that "the monthly deficits of "Lucifer" have been cheerfully borne by two of our brothers"?

We all suffer more or less, some of us are borne down by the complicated requirements, the senseless superfluities of social life. Might it not be worth some effort to introduce, even if only in our own immediate circle, a simpler mode of living. The saving thus effected in money, time, and health would enable us with ease to carry out our obligations to the T. S., and would, moreover, help to start a reformatory movement for the simplification of life that is a felt want in our day. Why do most of us find that there is such a small sum left when our personal expenses have been met to devote to public objects ? Is it that our tastes are luxurious, our palates difficult to satisfy, our vanity inordinate ? or is it that we have got into a social groove and will not take the trouble to get out of it — do not look ahead to see whither it is leading us?

Want of thought can hardly serve as a justification for a course of action that threatens to land us in practical, even though unintentional, selfishness.

Pleasant, social intercourse, dainty dinners, charming costumes are all very well in their way, but if they can only be indulged at the expense of work neglected, of unpaid subscriptions, of deafness to the call of duty, they cost more than they are worth.

But what is our duty, some may say ? Are we not to indulge our legitimate tastes and fancies?

Yes, decidedly, so that they are legitimate. But let us be practical, let us compare relative values. Money is powerful, but it cannot be spent in two ways at once. What do members of the T. S. want to do ? If they wish to aid in the establishment of a universal brotherhood of humanity, they must themselves act in a fraternal manner. Now, surely it is no brotherly action to spend money upon personal indulgences while surrounded by starving thousands. And thousands are starving, not only for the food that goes to nourish the body, but for the knowledge that should nourish the mind. Others, again, and their name is legion, are kept in a state of semi-starvation for the want of that blessed leisure which alone can enable them to partake of the nourishment around them. It is not only the overwrought seamstress, or the sweater's victim, that pines in the midst of plenty, from sheer inability to snatch sufficient time to satisfy the craving of mind and spirit. Many a man in the pursuit of wealth has converted himself into a machine. He eats and sleeps to keep himself going, but all his energies are exhausted in the fatal, frantic struggle to get the wherewithal to keep up his suburban villa, clothe his wife and daughters, send his son to college, and leave behind enough to enable his womankind to perpetuate the useless existence to which they have been trained. And these same women, are they more fortunate? Have they more leisure ? Not at all. Their lives are consumed in a long, unceasing effort to make a hundred pounds do the work of two. To this they dedicate their lives, to this they sacrifice their health, their temper, or nerves, as the case may be; for this they become deaf to the cry of the distressed needlewoman — cheap clothes they must and will have — the plaint of the never-finished domestic. It has become a "duty", — might we not almost say *the duty*, to make a "good appearance", and many women are giving up all that elevates and consecrates a home for its fulfilment.

Of late years we have heard a great deal about dress reform and food reform, but the motive power to give vitality to the movement has been wanting. As long as we are living for ourselves chiefly, it is of no great consequence that our time and our forces are wasted in. one. way rather than in another; but when we realize that the hunger and nakedness of the destitute are demanding of each one of us a remedy, then we feel that the time and money spent on our frills and flounces mean the shivering of some half-clad child, who might have been warmly clothed with that which has been spent upon our superfluities, the matter receives another aspect. The same with food reform. We may become vegetarians, and think that this is enough, but this we do for the purification of our personal system, and with no regard to its effect on our neighbours; if, being vegetarians, we require elaborate dishes that take long hours to prepare, we do little or nothing to solve the problem of how to get food to the hungry. Some small saving in the cost of living we do effect, but if this is balanced against a great expenditure of labour in the preparation of food, it should not be enough to satisfy Theosophists. Nothing but the least possible expenditure upon mere personal gratification should content those who feel that to feed and clothe others is as imperative a duty as to clothe and feed ourselves. At least this should be so in the existing state of the world, when hunger and degradation, that money might lessen, are suffered by thousands. If to share one's last loaf is the duty of a Theosophist, surely it is a not less urgent duty so to order the daily life that the blessings of enlightenment may be shared with as many as possible. Duty, we read in the "Key to Theosophy", is "that which is due to humanity, to our fellowmen, neighbours, family, and especially that which we owe to all those who are poorer and more helpless than we are ourselves". This is the debt which, if left unpaid during life, leaves us spiritually insolvent and moral bankrupts in our next incarnation. These are solemn words, and it may seem to some that the little details of daily life are too insignificant to be treated with solemnity, but let such reflect that the noblest, most heroic life is made up of trivial details that win their grand total only when the final account is rendered.

THEOSOPHY IN DAILY LIFE

by J. Campbell Ver Planck

READING in the Sacred Books of the East, I came upon these lines:—

"He lets his mind pervade one quarter of the world with thoughts of Love, and so the second, and so the third, and so the fourth. And thus the whole wide world, above, below. around and everywhere, does he continue to pervade with heart of Love, far reaching grown great and beyond measure.

"Just as a mighty trumpeter makes himself heard, and that without difficulty — in all the four directions — even so of all things that have shape or life, there is not one that he passes by or leaves aside, but regards them all with mind set free, and deep-felt Love. Verily this is the way to a state of union with Brahma.

"And he lets his mind pervade one quarter of the world with thoughts of pity, sympathy and equanimity, and so the second, and so the third, and so the fourth. And thus the whole round world, above, below, around and everywhere, does he continue to pervade with heart of pity, sympathy, and equanimity, far reaching, grown great and beyond measure."

For this Scriptural injunction there is, of course, a reason; The mighty energy thus diffused through space not only attracts the divine, but it gives, it informs, it creates. On every plane it has its perfect work. On the highest, it becomes the messenger of the Perfect Law which is a Law of Love. Its processes can be scientifically considered and demonstrated in Theosophical thought. Its rule and subjection of the lower astral plane can be clearly shown. But what seems to concern us most with the opening of a new year, is its effect on the plane best known to the average man, or its application in daily life.

As Theosophists, we have given our adherence to the principles of Universal Brotherhood and a search for Truth. The most indifferent member of our Society has still signed such a pledge, calling his word of honour to attest its reality. Some of us have gone much further than this. A consideration which presents itself to all alike, a reality which is no respecter of persons, is this: Are we or are we not conforming to the spirit and letter of that pledge? Are we endeavouring to form a *real* Brotherhood? I do not need to point out that intellectual enlightenment is only a means, and one of several means, to that benign end. It will be apparent to any thinking person that the intellectual germs which are the bearers of Truth must sprout and bear in our lives; must be transformed into deeds and thoughts impersonal, fraternal, and informed with universal love, or else they are mere withered husks which only encumber the mind that has received them. We may send our literature into every home; we may find our facts upon every man's tongue; and still our Society will be an utter failure as a vital, living Brotherhood if the spirit and activity of universal Love is not infused into it. No one can so infuse it but ourselves. Each individual is responsible for its absence, if it be absent, for it alone adequately represents our pledge. We have not given the attestation of our honour to a mere formalism, but to a Reality; to an unlimited energic Charity, without which we are indeed as brass and tinkling cymbals.

Hence no more urgent question now presents itself to the earnest student (or even to those whose "honour" keeps its pledges) than this one, namely: How shall I convert this philosophy into a working force which shall prove useful in daily life ? It is true that the Theosophical code of ethics, were it followed by every individual, would change the face of the world in a day. It also follows that such influence must be of the greatest practical as well as moral use. If each one of us believed that every wrong done would as surely react upon us as that a ball thrown against a wall will rebound, and that what injures one man injures all, it is certain that all our ways of living and thinking would change, and that we should enter a wider sphere, a larger spirit of Life. We should then experience a spiritual, ethical, and practical consolidation or Brotherhood.

At the same time, this study and personal practice of the philosophy does not wholly fulfil our pledge. We are still in the world; its ties are more or less interwoven with our daily life, and for this world as it now stands we are largely responsible. All about us are wrongs and sorrows which only a change in the inner nature of mankind can exterminate. We know this change is far off in point of time and concerns the race, while our own personal efforts show us how difficult is its accomplishment. It is indeed not to be accomplished until we regard the entire universe with thoughts of Equanimity and Love. What then shall we do ? Shall we wait patiently for this change, striving meanwhile to lift ourselves and such comrades as may be drawn to hear our words to a higher inner life ? If we do this much only, the change will never come. We have taken up the attitude of separation unconsciously, and the estranged world feels that we have deserted it in a need which the soul realizes, though the individual may not. In the inner attitude we are to stand aloof from the fever, the doubt, the selfishness, and carnival of desire; but the outer man must also fulfil his duty, and he does that by drawing close to his fellowmen and by working among them. Until the intuition of the race shall be more highly developed, men need to see our personal presence and activity before they can realize our spiritual sympathy. Just as we give object-lessons to a child, so our work explains to them the reality of our pledge and belief.

Spiritual advancement is not a result of mechanical (so to call it) cyclic progress, nor yet a result of the will of the gods. The progress of Law must be reinforced by human will and effort before the personal soul can be benefited by it. The way of the race is devious and long; it is accomplished through individual effort, and each real reform in institutions, in morals, in every department of Life, brings us one step nearer the goal. These things, external though they appear, may each be made the vehicle of higher powers, through the energy of universal Love. As witnesses to the expanding heart of man and to the vital growth of his belief in human and divine consolidation, they bring us inwardly as well as outwardly into closer relations with one another.

There are of course exceptions in the cases of persons who through their inward fitness have been called away from the world to enter upon a special-course of training and service which shall fit them for duties upon other lines and planes than those known to individual life. All such persons have, at some time, worked ardently in the primary fields, and have, through such work, developed into more impersonal and more divine uses. They stood once where we now stand, and through proportional efforts in all directions, they have passed on. It is our part to follow them, and while we are still in the world we may be sure that a part of our work lies in it, and includes every practical as well as every spiritual effort towards realizing the highest conception of Universal Brotherhood.

There are many Theosophists who do not grasp the urgency of this question concerning the utilization of Theosophy in daily life. Perhaps some of them feel their own ignorance, their unfitness to teach, and wait to know more before they speak to other men. They forget that he who cannot teach can work. Our work teaches. Moreover, through unselfish work we are taught. To learn intellectually, some may wait in vain; and indeed none will truly learn in any sense until they convert what little they do know into working force, just as our food is useless to us until its digestion has set free some amount of nervous energy, for whose translation into work Nature herself provides. All these natural processes are copies of those of the spiritual world, and thus all things bear witness to that Truth which is their Being. Other Theosophists are struggling with material cares; others do not stop to think of the real bearing of their professions of Brotherhood. In short, as many reasons for indifference prevail as were sent to the Biblical King when he bade his neighbours come to the wedding feast. Still, I believe the chief of these is the want of co-ordinated thought. Not so long ago an earnest student wrote to the American Headquarters to say that through an appeal made to him for assistance in some work which was being done he had come to realize the necessity of such work and the lack of it that he was sure many others, like himself, were so preoccupied by daily cares that they had not waked up to the importance of helping the Theosophical movement in some direction, and he offered money to print an edition of a tract addressed to indifferent Theosophists, if some one would write it. These pages are the outcome, in second remove, of that work which stimulated him. As we light a fire by communicating to it the vibrations of a flame, so contact with the earnest effort of another sets free a corresponding and latent energy in the heart prepared for higher development.

These considerations are all the more pressing today. We are nearing the end of the cycle, and all events move more rapidly. Effort made now will have a far greater result than it would have later on. The momentum of a moving object depends upon the energy expended at its start, and those Theosophists, who are sufficiently intuitive to take advantage of cyclic currents and to work ardently with them and with the Great Powers, will find that they have laid up treasures there, where, to quote Emerson, compound interest is the rate of the exchequer. The credit of this exchequer is not personal man, but Humanity: what we give as individuals is repaid to the race. This is just, for from that race we spring in part. One year's work done now may fructify far more rapidly for this cause which is our own, than might ten years' work done at a less propitious time. It is true that materiality is now at its highest rate of progress, but with a latent downward tendency; while spiritual activity is accelerating with an upward tendency due to the present curve of progress. Can we doubt which will prevail ? It is now in our power to secure the prevalence of spiritual activity in individual lives, just as the Law has already provided for its prevalence in the Universal Scheme. There is scarcely one of us so poor that he cannot make some willing sacrifice, or has not some time or energy to give. Quantity does not matter so much as quality; it is the spirit of unselfish Love that works all wonders.

These thoughts accepted, the student asks himself where he shall begin, to what work lay his hand. For his personal life he alone can answer. If he be a member of the Theosophical Society, it will be well for him to work with and through his Branch; the greater the centre the greater the energy. Energy is proportionate to the square of the numbers producing it. The sum of energy produced by three united persons is nine times as great as that evolved by a single person. This ratio is due to the correlations of the forces employed. Where Theosophists have not joined the Society, they would do well to reflect on these facts. We are responsible for our latent possibilities. If we neglect to develop and enlarge them by joining a body pledged to Humanity, we must certainly be losers by our determined attitude of separation. We owe ourselves to others, if only for the encouragement of our external presence and support.

Turning our attention from individuals to the corporate Body itself, we find that we are reproached, and justly reproached, with doing little, if any, practical work. As we do not believe in indiscriminate missionary labours and argumentative conversion, we must seek other fields. Are there no children among us to be rescued from the doubts and confusion of our time ? Where are our Branch Sunday Schools, where music, story and object teaching of spirit through natural lessons, may give the little ones a happy and valued hour? Where are our Branch free libraries, with one member told off weekly to attend them, open of an evening to all comers ? Can we do nothing to help those social outcasts, so rarely rescued by formal religion, because, " the deed of virtue is without the love that should shine through it". It is vain to try to stop those who are on the fatally swift descent of sin, by assurances that some other, however divine, is responsible for them. If we can grapple their minds with the thought that they themselves are their own saviours and that we are integrally and actually their Brothers and Sisters, then indeed we may recover lost ground for the race. Everywhere great questions and great issues are confronting us and in some one of these each Branch should have a share. Not only should we join with outsiders in such good deeds as they have found to do, but we ought to have some distinctively Theosophical work of our own, first as individuals, next as Branches. For example, the competitive struggle and system of monopolies are working as much — if not more — injury as the use of intoxicating liquors. Everywhere thinkers of benevolent aspirations are inaugurating co-operative colonies or works. One such is the Credit Foncier of Sinaloa, a colony established in Mexico on co-operative principles, having excellent privileges from the Mexican Government. The colonists own the land, railroads and industries in common. All public property is so held, but the home is a private institution. The colony is governed by a body of elected Directors. The women vote equally with the men. No corporate churches are allowed; each man is free to worship as he may please in his own home. No intoxicating drinks are made or sold; no gambling or other houses of ill-repute allowed within the colony precincts. All persons are employed by the colony itself; labour is interchanged, and the net gain is divided among colonists according to their shares of stock. This is, perhaps, the largest co-operative venture ever made, and has unprecedented advantages of harbour, situation and climate; but, above all, its ethical principles are integral and vital. At one time a colonist wrote on behalf of a betrayed and deserted woman, against whom the doors of our civilization were closed, when she tried to return to the path of moral duty. The directors promptly responded by the gift of a share of stock and the assurance that all who endeavoured to live honestly and in a spirit of true fraternity were welcome to Sinaloa whatever might be the mistakes of their past. No more

Theosophical deed than this is known to me. It would seem as if colonies founded upon a more liberal and just division of labour and profit, upon a more enlightened system of interchange and interdependence, would tend to facilitate the advance of the race. All persons may not be able to join them, but they can help them. Clubs are already founded to assist co-operation, and such might be started in Branches interested in seeing justice established as the regulator of human institutions. It is not division of property that the honest man wants, but a division of labour and profits other than that awarded by a system which regards money as the chief factor of prosperity, and energy — the great life force — as its underling and slave. While I am well aware that physical energy is but one division of that life force, as regards the value of such energy and that expended for the amassing of personal wealth and for personal and selfish indulgences, I submit that the former is far higher than the latter and should not be underpaid. *The motive determines the value and quality of energy as well as the Plane on which it operates.* That other Theosophists think with me is proved by the interest of others in co-operative principles, while the fact that these principles, and the life they give rise to, lead thoughtful minds into a more distinctly Theosophical line of thought, is evidenced by two directors and some members of the above-mentioned colony having joined the T. S.. Godin, the great co-operator of Guise, also became a Theosophist.

These are some of the opportunities of work which present themselves, and which may be carried on at the same time with that inward work of self-conquest and self-purification undertaken in the silence of the heart by all true students. I would urge that this subject of Theosophical work be held under special consideration at our next annual convention. The time has come for us to make good our pledge; to ask ourselves whether we shall be a Brotherhood in every vital sense, a working army united by a harmonious, charitable, unprejudiced spirit of sympathy and love, or a mere formal organization interested in intellectual pursuits. Let each one of us ask himself this question, and

43

ask until he finds the, answer: Am I working to the full extent of my powers and in every possible direction for that Universal Brotherhood to which I am pledged, and in whose future realization I implicitly believe — witness my "word of honour" ? Else honour, loyalty, and Brotherhood are empty echoes of an idle and fantastic dream.

www.ingramcontent.com/pod-product-compliance
Lightning Source LLC
La Vergne TN
LVHW041501070426
835507LV00009B/749